Make Your Own Squishies

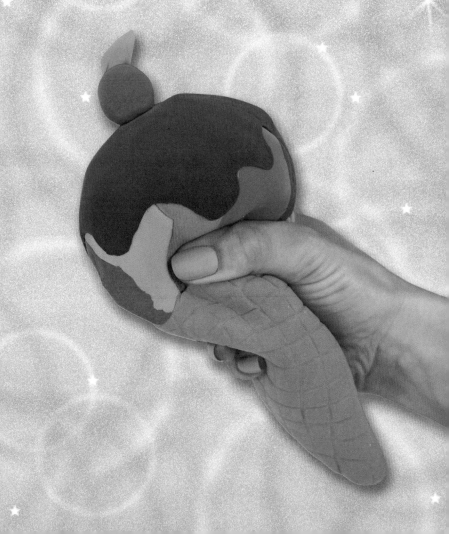

Make Your Own Squishies

15 Slow–Rise & Smooshy Projects for You To Create

Stacia Ann

FOR YOUNG READERS

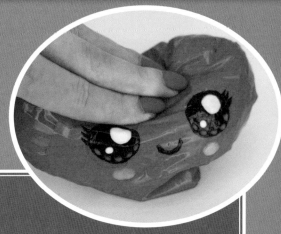

TABLE OF CONTENTS

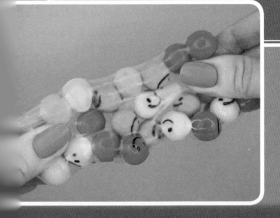

DISCLAIMER

The projects suggested in this book can be potentially hazardous. They should not be attempted without adult supervision. Some of these materials pose a choking hazard or can be toxic if ingested or inhaled. Additionally, certain materials and tools in this project are potentially hazardous if used incorrectly or mishandled, and should be handled only by adults with caution and great care.

INTRODUCTION

Squishy toys have become increasingly popular these days. People from different countries, both kids and adults, contribute to their expanding variety. This is of no surprise because squishies are great means to fight stress, and this is the reason why throughout the book I will refer to them as "anti-stress" toys.

However, it's not quite correct to refer to these products exclusively as toys. There is a category of them that combines the squishy body with an actually useful feature, as it is done with squishy pens, lamps, trinkets—you name it!

Certainly, while originating from Japan, these anti-stress toys changed both in form and content as they were adapted by other countries and cultures. The materials, the ways we make squishies, and the usage scenarios vary throughout the world.

At present, a squishy toy can be made from some factory-made material or from common household items. The exterior and functional areas are left entirely to the designer's discretion. That being said, squishies provide opportunities in a wonderfully simple way to unleash one's creativity and direct it into something fun and satisfying.

This book contains fifteen do-it-yourself projects to get you started with squishy toys. Most of the tutorials show you the ways to utilize resources at hand. There are, however, instructions on how to handle factory-made synthetic squishy materials. Regardless of material or approach, all of them are colorful, fun, and great anti-stress toys!

Don't try these projects without adult supervision. Never place any small objects in your mouth. Some materials can be toxic if you contact, inhale, or eat them. Also, tools can be potentially hazardous if used incorrectly.

1. MAGICAL UNICORN DONUT

What could be better than a donut? Only a donut in the form of a unicorn, of course! This toy is extremely cute and popular. Let's learn how to make it with our own hands.

Materials

- 1 sheet of cardboard
- 1 block of memory foam or 1 sponge
- Air-dry clay (white, yellow, pink, purple, and green)
- PVA glue
- Glitter
- Black and pink fabric paint

1 It is best to start by preparing a cardboard template.

2 Take a block of memory foam or a sponge (for a squishy effect, it is better to use a block of memory foam) and draw a donut following the outline of the template.

3 Take the scissors and cut all the way around, removing any excess foam around the shape that you just drew. (Caution: Scissors are sharp! Please use care when handling scissors and do so under adult supervision.)

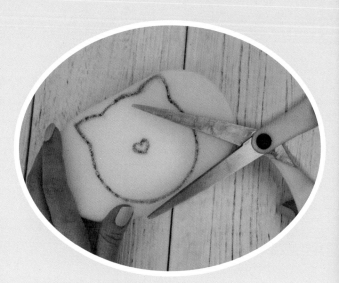

4 Make sure your donut is as smooth as possible; you need to use your scissors to sort of "shave away" all the little outstanding bits and edges. Don't worry if your donut is not an ideal form; soon, we'll hide all the imperfections.

5 Use a rolling pin to flatten some modeling air-dry clay. Even after this kind of clay dries it still stays soft, so it's great for a squishy toy.

6 Cover the sponge with clay. Try to make the cover layer as smooth as possible. Don't forget to remove any excess clay.

7 Roll out some more yellow clay.

8 Fold the clay thread in half and twist to create the unicorn's horn.

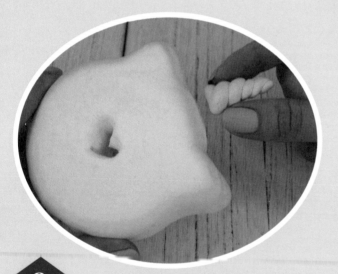

9 Stick the horn to the toy. For this we do not need any glue, since both of the clay elements have not dried yet and will adhere to one another.

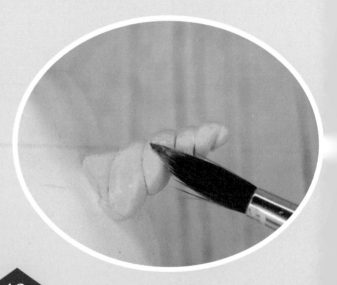

10 Apply some PVA glue to the horn.

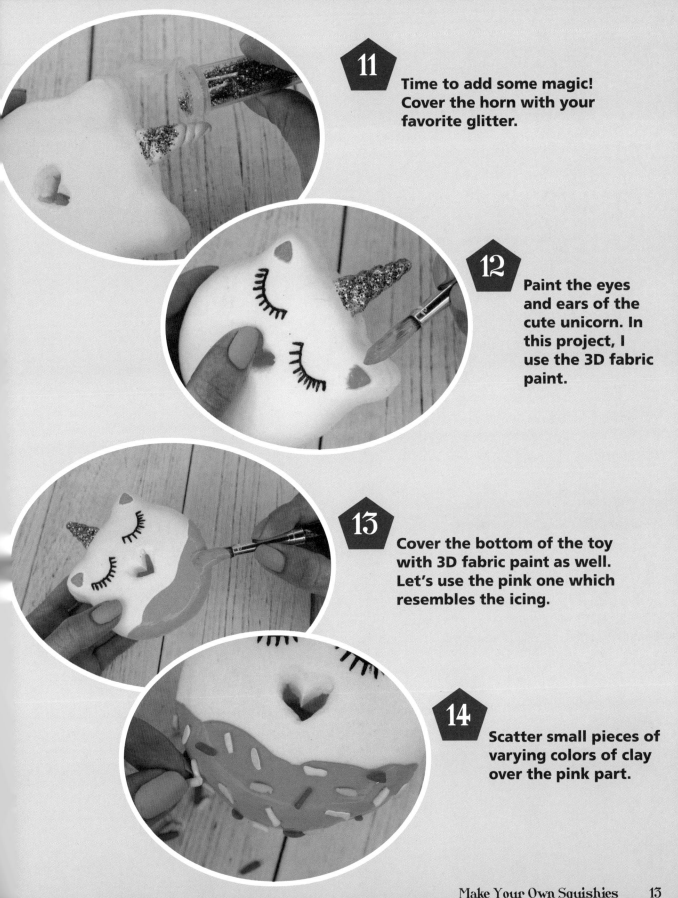

11 Time to add some magic! Cover the horn with your favorite glitter.

12 Paint the eyes and ears of the cute unicorn. In this project, I use the 3D fabric paint.

13 Cover the bottom of the toy with 3D fabric paint as well. Let's use the pink one which resembles the icing.

14 Scatter small pieces of varying colors of clay over the pink part.

Let's add some decoration. Roll and form some pink and violet air-dry clay into spheres.

To make roses, take a pink circle and twist it.

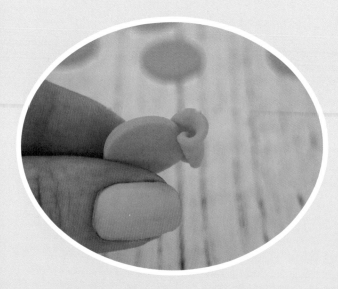

Then attach another circle to it, and repeat this until all the rose petals are formed.

18

Glue the roses around the horn.

Let the toy fully dry overnight and then you can play with this cute unicorn donut!

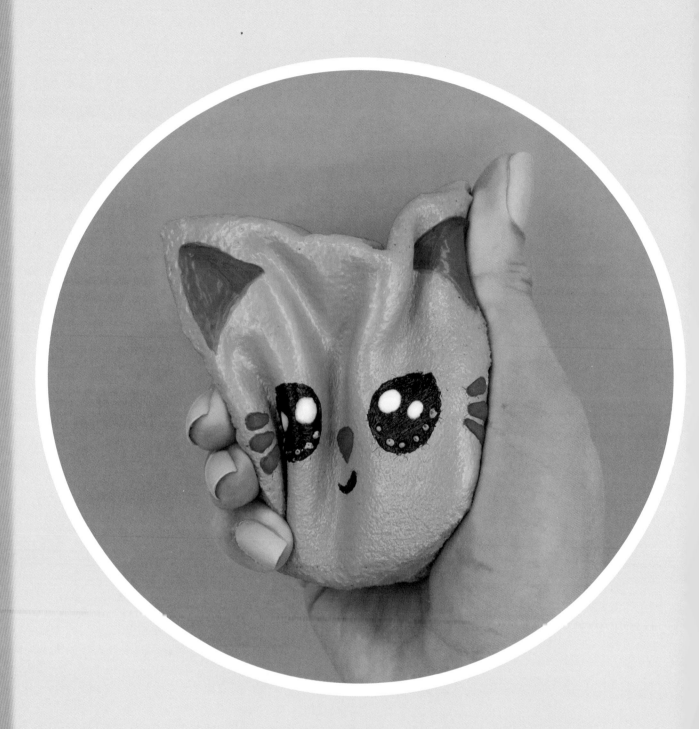

Don't try these projects without adult supervision. Never place any small objects in your mouth. Some materials can be toxic if you contact, inhale, or eat them. Also, tools can be potentially hazardous if used incorrectly.

2. CUTE CAT

Painting a sponge is one of the easiest ways to make a squishy toy, so let's make this toy in the form of what everyone likes . . . yes, a kitty cat!

Materials

- 1 sheet of paper
- 1 block of memory foam or 1 sponge
- Acrylic paint (blue, black, white, pink, and purple)
- Transparent glue or PVA glue

1 For convenience, you can use the image to the left as a template.

2 Using the template, draw a cat outline on a block of memory foam or a sponge (for squishy effect, it is better to use a block of memory foam).

3 Cut all the way around the drawing. Remove all the excess around the shape that you just drew. Make sure the surface of the block you used is as smooth as possible; you need to "shave away" all the little excess bits and edges.
(Caution: Scissors are sharp! Please use them under adult supervision.)

4 Mix blue acrylic paint and transparent glue or PVA glue in a 1:1 ratio. Also, as an option, you can use 3D fabric paint.

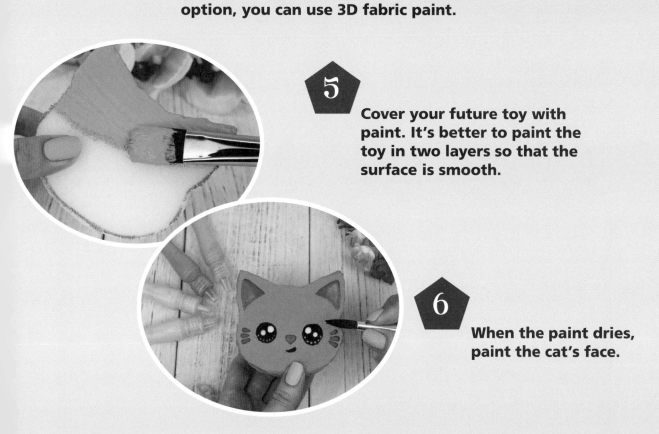

5 Cover your future toy with paint. It's better to paint the toy in two layers so that the surface is smooth.

6 When the paint dries, paint the cat's face.

After everything has dried, the toy is ready for use!

Don't try these projects without adult supervision. Never place any small objects in your mouth. Some materials can be toxic if you contact, inhale, or eat them. Also, tools can be potentially hazardous if used incorrectly.

3. Panda

Foam sheets are great craft material for a variety of projects, and squishy toys are no exception. So, let's make a super-soft panda using this material.

Materials

- 1 white foam sheet
- A spherical vase, a deep plate, or a similar container
- 1 black foam sheet
- Hot glue or superglue
- 1 plastic bag
- Acrylic paints (blue, white, and pink)

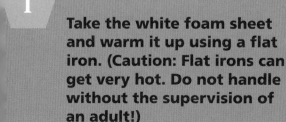

1 Take the white foam sheet and warm it up using a flat iron. (Caution: Flat irons can get very hot. Do not handle without the supervision of an adult!)

2 For the next step, you can use a spherical vase, a deep plate, or a similar container.

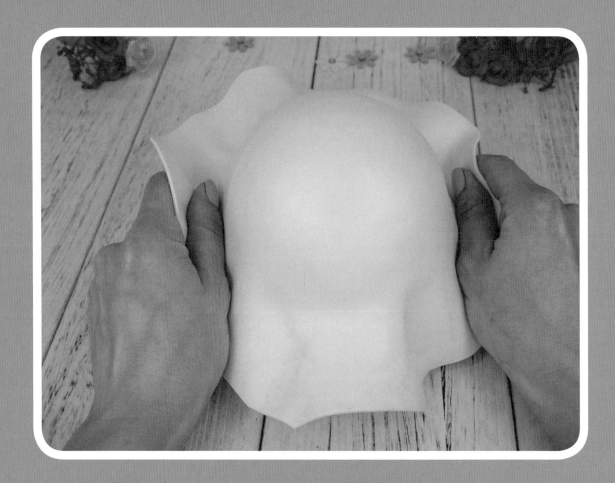

3

While the sheet is still warm, quickly put it in a deep plate or vase and stretch the foam sheet. You will probably have to apply some force. The goal of this step is to make the sheet take the shape of the container.

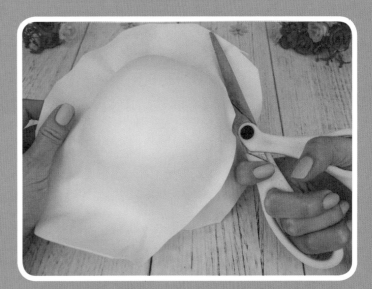

4

Cut all the excess around. (Caution: Scissors are sharp! Please use under adult supervision.)

5

Glue the edges of the foam sphere onto a flat piece of white foam sheet but leave a part of an edge intact. You can use hot glue or superglue. (Caution: Hot glue guns are dangerous. Do not use without the supervision of an adult.)

6

After this, you will have formed a "pocket" as shown in the picture.

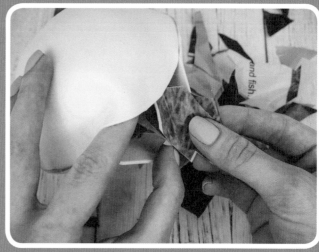

7

Cut up any plastic bag. This will be a filling for the toy.

8

Put the pieces of the plastic bag in the "pocket."

9

Glue the toy's edge to the other, closing up the pocket's hole.

10

Cut all the excess that might be left around the edges. (Caution: Scissors are sharp! Please use under adult supervision.)

11 Cut ears from a black foam sheet and glue to the Panda's head.

12 Cut out the elements of the panda's face, including the eyes, nose, and mouth. Pandas are black and white, so you can use the same black foam sheet to do this.

13 Glue all elements to the toy.

14 Paint details on the eyes and ears with acrylic paints. Let it dry before use!

Don't try these projects without adult supervision. Never place any small objects in your mouth. Some materials can be toxic if you contact, inhale, or eat them. Also, tools can be potentially hazardous if used incorrectly.

4. Rainbow Ice Cream

Caution! This is extremely yummy looking, but do not eat this project! This time we will make a large multicolored ice cream cone with chocolate and a cherry on top.

Materials

- Cotton
- 1 plastic bag
- Tape
- Air-dry clay (violet, blue, brown, green, yellow, and red)

1

Stuff some cotton in the corner of the plastic bag.

2

Form the bag into a cone.

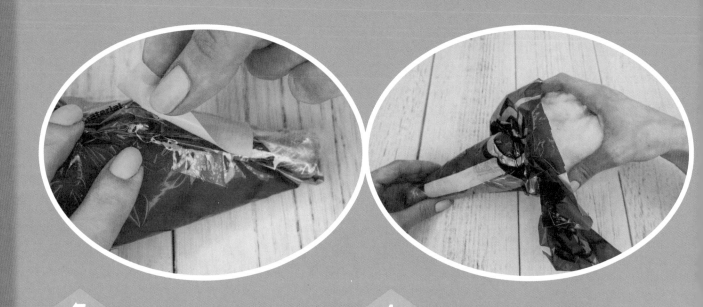

Close it up using tape.

4 **Put a ball made of cotton on the top of the cone.**

5 **Cover the cotton ball with a bag and close it up with tape. This shape should resemble something like an ice cream cone.**

Roll out and join together some violet, blue, green, yellow, and red air-dry clay. Alternatively, you can buy just white clay and change the color using acrylic paints or food coloring.

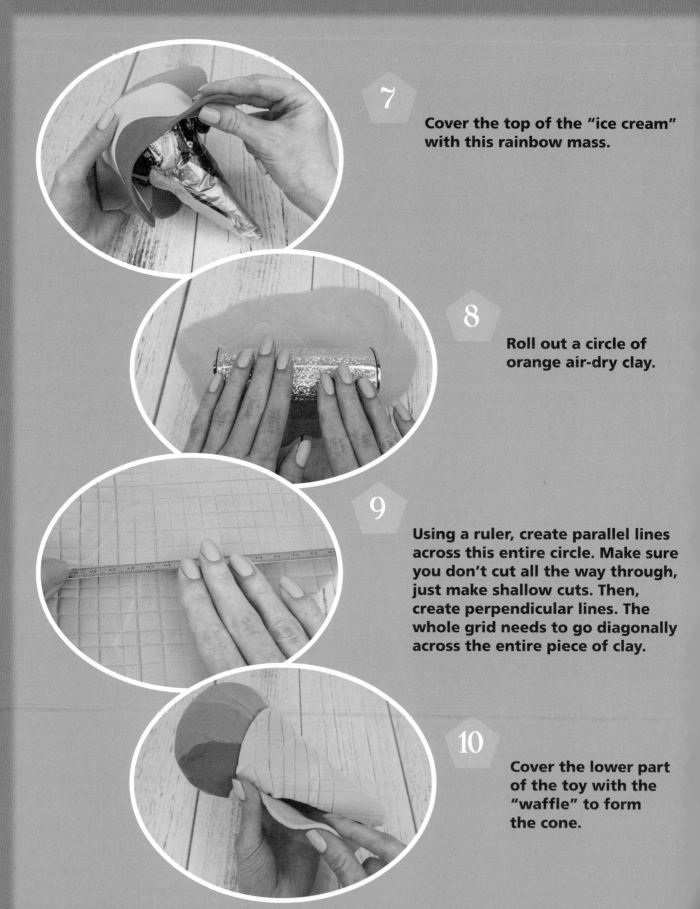

7

Cover the top of the "ice cream" with this rainbow mass.

8

Roll out a circle of orange air-dry clay.

9

Using a ruler, create parallel lines across this entire circle. Make sure you don't cut all the way through, just make shallow cuts. Then, create perpendicular lines. The whole grid needs to go diagonally across the entire piece of clay.

10

Cover the lower part of the toy with the "waffle" to form the cone.

11 At the top, put a ball of brown air-dry clay that will resemble chocolate syrup.

12 From the same kind of clay, form a green leaf. Just pinch and flatten an oval until you have a sort of eye shape—or, in fact, a leaf shape! Using the pad of your thumb, very gently rub over the top of the leaf surface. This will help to get rid of your fingerprints.

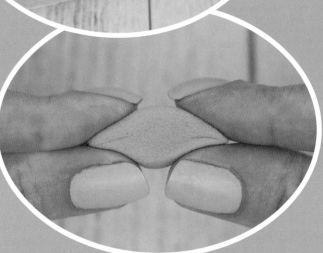

13 Put the leaf on a red ball of air-dry clay, which will resemble a cherry.

14 Add the cherry to the top of your ice cream cone.

Give the toy a day to dry and it's ready to play with!

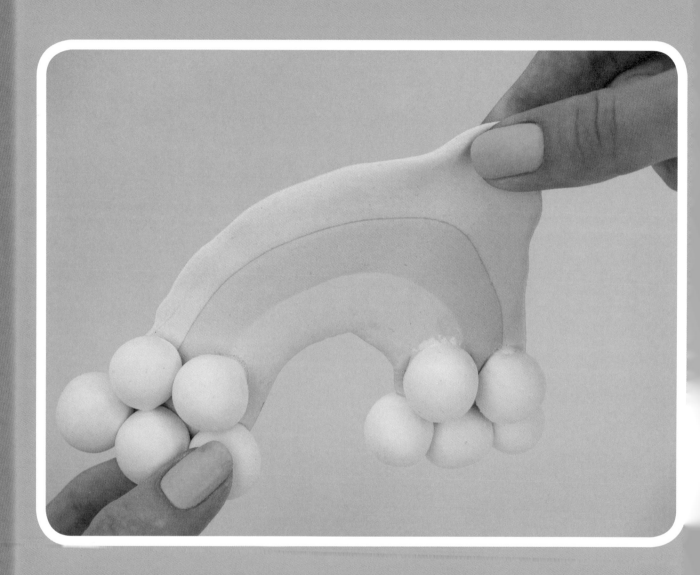

Don't try these projects without adult supervision. Never place any small objects in your mouth. Some materials can be toxic if you contact, inhale, or eat them. Also, tools can be potentially hazardous if used incorrectly.

5. PASTEL RAINBOW

Sometimes you don't need a complex recipe to make a squishy. In fact, it only takes some moisturized air-dry clay to create one.

Materials
- Water
- Baby oil
- Silicone
- Acrylic paint or food coloring (white, pink, purple, and blue)

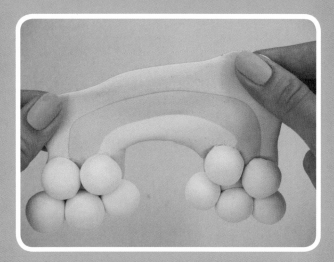

1

Pour some water and oil in a 1:1 ratio into a container. You can use any oil, but baby oil is best.

2

Next comes the silicone. You can buy this in any hardware store.

3

Mix all the ingredients in the container for about thirty seconds.

4

Squeeze the liquid out from the silicon and mash it with your hand.

5

Divide the resulting mass into four parts.

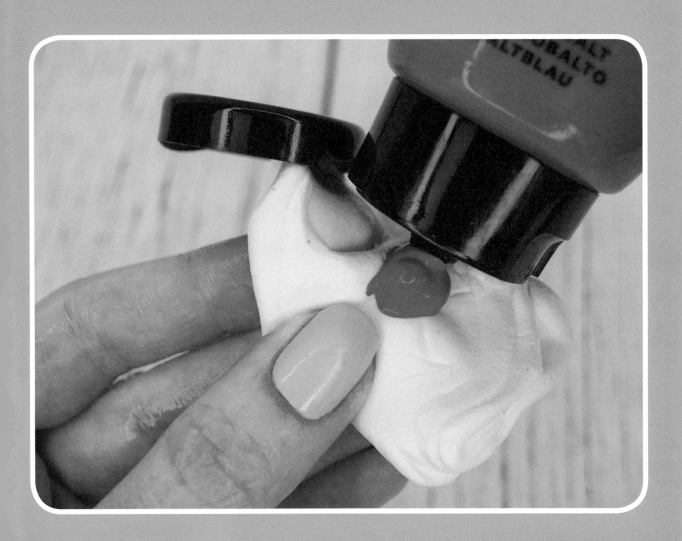

6

Add color to each mass with acrylic paint or food coloring.

7

When you're finished, you should have a white, pink, purple, and blue part.

8

Roll out the pink, purple, and blue pieces. You need to get something like a string of every part.

9

Put these together and form a rainbow. Because the mass has not dried yet, it will stick together.

10 Make balls from the white mass.

11 Connect white balls to the bottom edges of the rainbow to create clouds.

12 Before you start playing with it, apply baby powder to the surface and give a toy some time to dry (it will take about one to two hours).

Don't try these projects without adult supervision. Never place any small objects in your mouth. Some materials can be toxic if you contact, inhale, or eat them. Also, tools can be potentially hazardous if used incorrectly.

6. Green Apple

So, what about Orbeez? They are bouncy, crazy, and so satisfying. You can use them to reduce stress, so they are perfect for making an anti-stress toy. These instructions will show you how to create a cute apple Orbeez toy.

<table>
<tr><td>

Materials

- Parchment paper
- 2 sheets of vinyl
- Orbeez
- Green food coloring
- Green permanent marker
- 1 sheet of cardboard
- Clear tape
- Super glue

</td></tr>
</table>

Draw an apple template without a leaf on parchment paper with a pencil. An important thing to note is that you need to use parchment paper because it is heat-resistant.

Place the apple template between two sheets of vinyl.

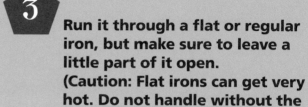

3 Run it through a flat or regular iron, but make sure to leave a little part of it open.
(Caution: Flat irons can get very hot. Do not handle without the supervision of an adult!)

4 Cut the excess vinyl from the apple's edges.
(Caution: Scissors are sharp! Please use under adult supervision.)

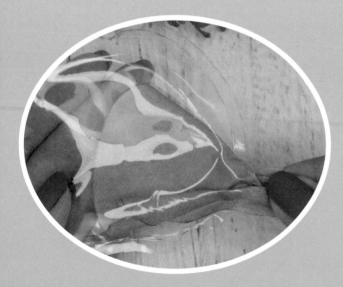

5 Remove the apple template.

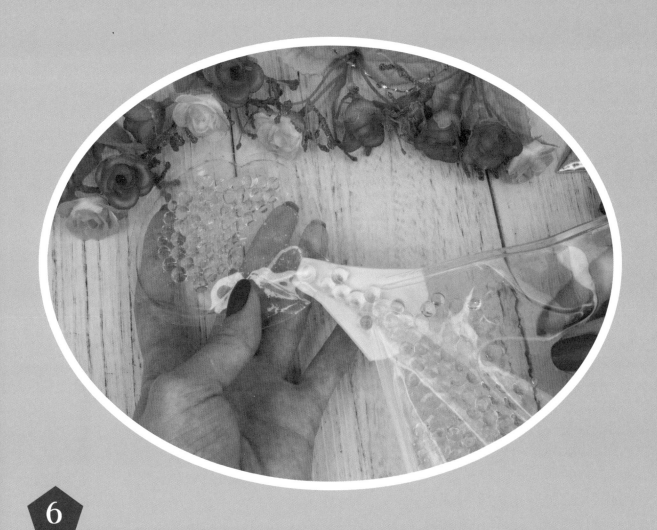

6

Fill the future toy with Orbeez using a paper funnel (just make a paper cone and cut an inverted V shape at the end of the cone to form the hole).

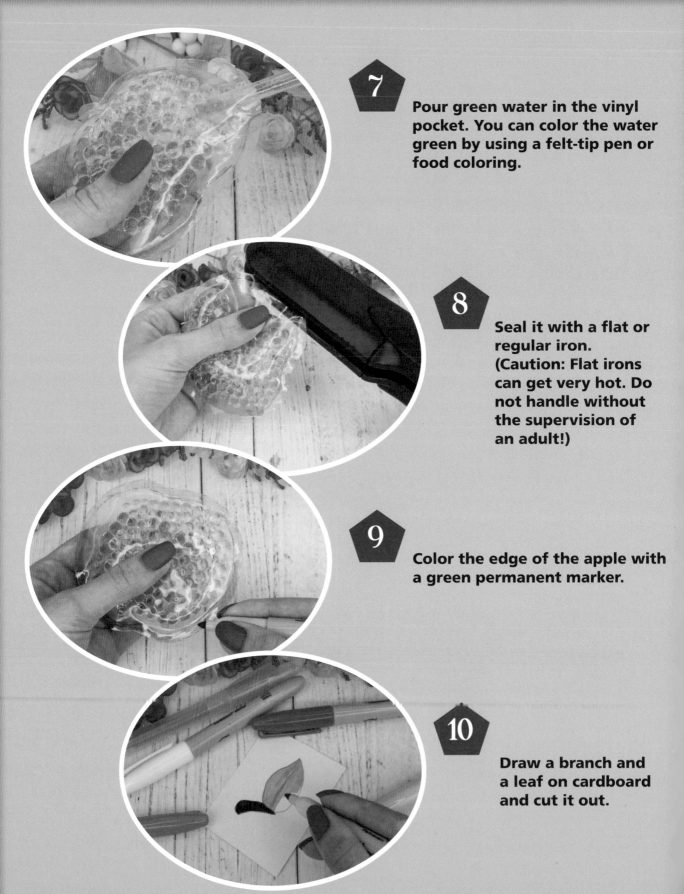

7 Pour green water in the vinyl pocket. You can color the water green by using a felt-tip pen or food coloring.

8 Seal it with a flat or regular iron. (Caution: Flat irons can get very hot. Do not handle without the supervision of an adult!)

9 Color the edge of the apple with a green permanent marker.

10 Draw a branch and a leaf on cardboard and cut it out.

18
Put some clear tape over the branch and the leaf. This will protect it from damage. After all this, just glue the painted branch with the leaf onto the toy using super glue.

This toy won't pop out when you squeeze it, but it's definitely calming and satisfying during a timeout.

Don't try these projects without adult supervision. Never place any small objects in your mouth. Some materials can be toxic if you contact, inhale, or eat them. Also, tools can be potentially hazardous if used incorrectly.

7. SMART COOKIE

Silicone is a great material from which you can make a lot of creative projects, and a slow-rising squishy toy is one of them.

Materials

- Corn starch
- 100 percent silicone
- Foil
- Acrylic paint or food coloring (black, brown, white, and yellow)
- Piece of paper
- Glue
- Cotton or substitute filling

 1 Put some corn starch into a container followed by some silicone. It's best to use 100 percent silicone, as it will produce a soft mass that does not harden very quickly. You may want to use rubber gloves for this step to keep your hands clean.

 2 Join these two components together to create the squishy mass. This should be colored with acrylic paint or food coloring. At this stage, it is better to use gloves because the mass may stick to your hands. If this happens, don't wash them, just wipe them with a napkin. Kitchen cleaning wipes are also perfect for removing silicone from the hands.

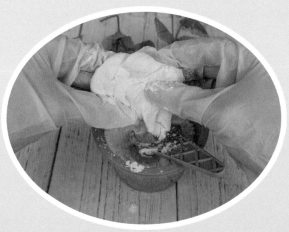

3 Prepare the parts of the squishy by adding food coloring and rolling the starch into separate black, brown, and yellow pieces. Make sure the yellow ball is larger than the other two.

4 Mold a 3D cookie template from tinfoil.

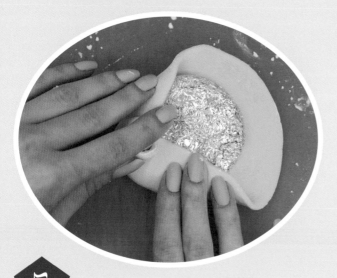

5 Make the yellow mass flat. Place the foil cookie template inside the mass and close it.

6 Draw on a piece of paper all the details: the eyes, the smile, and the glasses. This will be the template.

Flatten the black mass and according to the templates, draw and cut out all the details. (Caution: Scissors are sharp! Please use under adult supervision.)

Place the details on the cookie.

From the brown mass, make orbs of different sizes.

10

Place the spheres on the cookie and press down to adhere to the yellow sphere. Spread them out evenly so the cookie looks well-rounded.

Paint a cute face. It is better to use acrylic paint mixed with glue for this step.

12

After thirty minutes, the mass will harden. When this happens, carefully cut the yellow mass with scissors as shown.

13 Remove the foil template from the cookie.

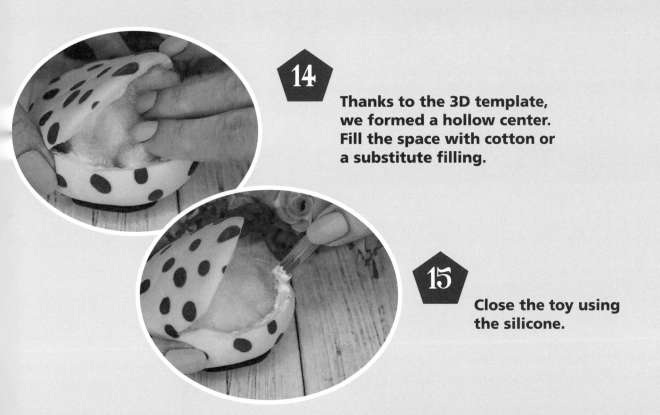

14 Thanks to the 3D template, we formed a hollow center. Fill the space with cotton or a substitute filling.

15 Close the toy using the silicone.

This toy is super soft to touch and looks good enough to eat!

Don't try these projects without adult supervision. Never place any small objects in your mouth. Some materials can be toxic if you contact, inhale, or eat them. Also, tools can be potentially hazardous if used incorrectly.

8. Piece of Cake

This slow-rising strawberry cake squishy is dedicated to your sweet tooth. This toy is easily made and looks amazing.

Materials

- 1 porous yellow sponge with shadowed pock marks
- 1 smooth white sponge
- Super glue
- Fabric paint (white and pink)
- Rubber bands
- 1 large bead or pom-pom

1

For this project, you need two types of sponge: porous yellow sponge with shadowed pock marks and a smooth white sponge. Cut out two triangular shapes from the porous sponge and another one from the smooth sponge. Don't forget to round off the rough edges to make the surface as smooth as possible. (Caution: Scissors are sharp! Please use under adult supervision.)

Apply super glue along the contour.

Glue together the three triangles with the smooth triangle in the middle.

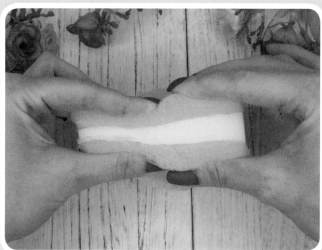

Use the fabric paint and paintbrushes to paint the squishy. Use a thick layer of yellow fabric paint on the top and bottom triangles.

5 Paint the center triangle white.

 6 Now, it's time to start painting the pink glaze (3D paint is excellent for this because it's sticky). To get the dripped look perfect on the sides, put the paint on bit by bit.

 7 While the paint is still wet, decorate the toy with sprinkles.

 8 The easiest way to make sprinkles is to cut small pieces of colored rubber bands.

You can also glue a large bead or pom-pom using super glue so it looks like a cherry on top.

Place your squishy toy on a sheet of parchment paper to dry overnight. After your sweet squishy toy is completely dry, enjoy playing with it! It may even look delicious enough to eat, but you should know that it's not edible.

Don't try these projects without adult supervision. Never place any small objects in your mouth. Some materials can be toxic if you contact, inhale, or eat them. Also, tools can be potentially hazardous if used incorrectly.

9. The Cutest Phone

If you want to create something a little more complex, then this project is for you. This is the cutest phone squishy around!

1

Take memory foam or any sponge and trim down the foam into phone shapes. Pinch the foam as you're cutting; this makes it easier for your scissors to pass through the dense material. This project requires the creation of two parts: the front of the phone and the bumper.

2

On both parts, cut a hole. The result should be as shown in the picture on the far right. (Caution: Scissors are sharp! Please use under adult supervision.)

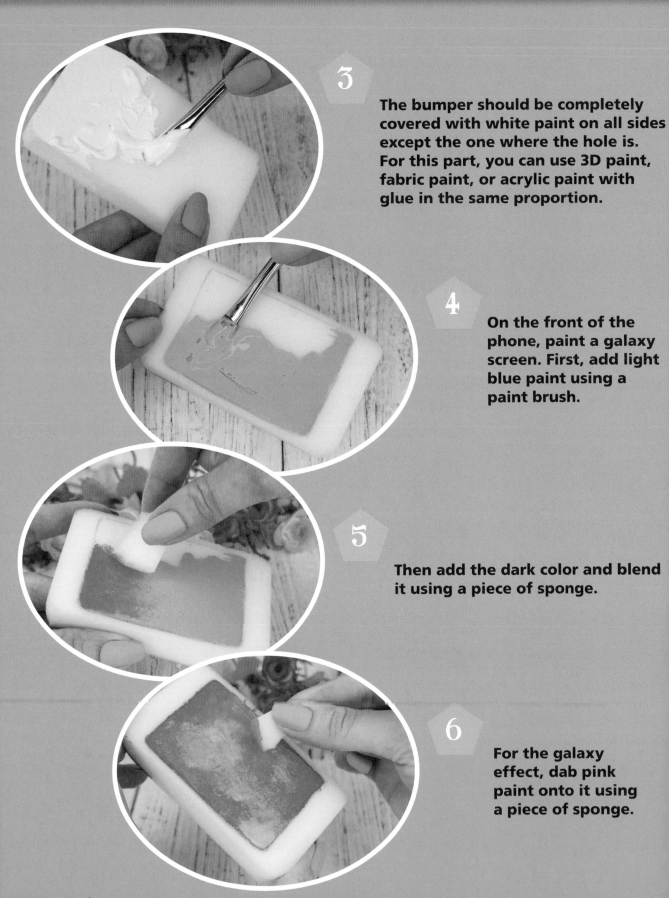

3

The bumper should be completely covered with white paint on all sides except the one where the hole is. For this part, you can use 3D paint, fabric paint, or acrylic paint with glue in the same proportion.

4

On the front of the phone, paint a galaxy screen. First, add light blue paint using a paint brush.

5

Then add the dark color and blend it using a piece of sponge.

6

For the galaxy effect, dab pink paint onto it using a piece of sponge.

7

While the paint is still wet, cover the screen with sparkles.

8

The entire sponge (aside from the screen) can now be coated with white paint.

9

Time to make the liquid part. To begin, pour transparent glue into a container.

10

Next, incorporate the same amount of water. Using a 1:1 ratio, create enough material to partially fill the balloon, as pictured on page 63.

11

Add to the mixture a bit of the glitter that you used on the cover of the screen.

12

Add borax into the container to create a slime that's stretchy and slightly watery.

13

Next, create a funnel with a water bottle by cutting off the top portion of the bottle.

14 Wrap a transparent balloon around the bottle.

15 Put the slime into the balloon.

16 This step is not mandatory, but it will make the toy more interesting and cute. Make a heart with a call icon using polymer clay and put it into the balloon.

17

Tie the balloon and cut off the end.

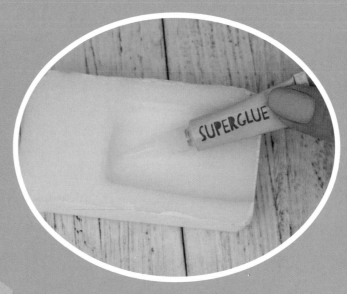

18

Apply a bit of glue in the cutout on the sponge.

19

Glue the balloon to the sponge, so that when you press the toy, the balloon does not pop out.

20

Apply super glue along the contour of the phone and glue together the front of the phone and the bumper.

21 All that's left is to draw the buttons using 3D paint or other paints that you used before.

After all the painted buttons are dry, you can play with the toy. When you squeeze it, the sparkling bubble pops out.

Don't try these projects without adult supervision. Never place any small objects in your mouth. Some materials can be toxic if you contact, inhale, or eat them. Also, tools can be potentially hazardous if used incorrectly.

10. KAWAII HEART

This project is one of the easiest and most accessible. Let's not forget that it's adorable! Using common household items, we will make a slow-rising kawaii heart squishy toy.

Materials

- 1 plastic bag
- Red sticky tape
- Glue
- Acrylic paint (blue, white, and black)

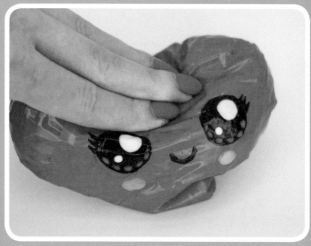

First, find any plastic bag and cut off one of the corners. (Caution: Scissors are sharp! Please use under adult supervision.)

2

From the corner, form a triangle which will be held together with adhesive tape.

 Cut some small pieces off of the plastic. The pieces will serve as a filling for the toy.

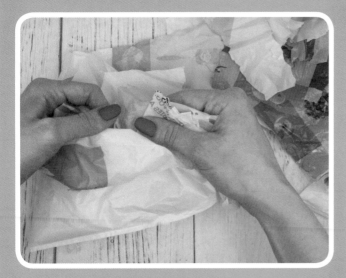

 Fill the plastic triangle with the filling you just made.

 From the plastic triangle, fold the top open end down to form the heart shape and close it with adhesive tape.

6

Now we need red sticky tape. Start with the top and stick it all around the heart shape. To make the toy look as neat and as even as possible, add two layers of tape.

7

Mix each of the acrylic paints with glue in an equal proportion. Form a few separate colors to use for the heart's facial details.

8

Paint a super cute face with the mixture.

Wait twenty-four hours for the paint on the toy to dry. After that, it is ready to play with and enjoy.

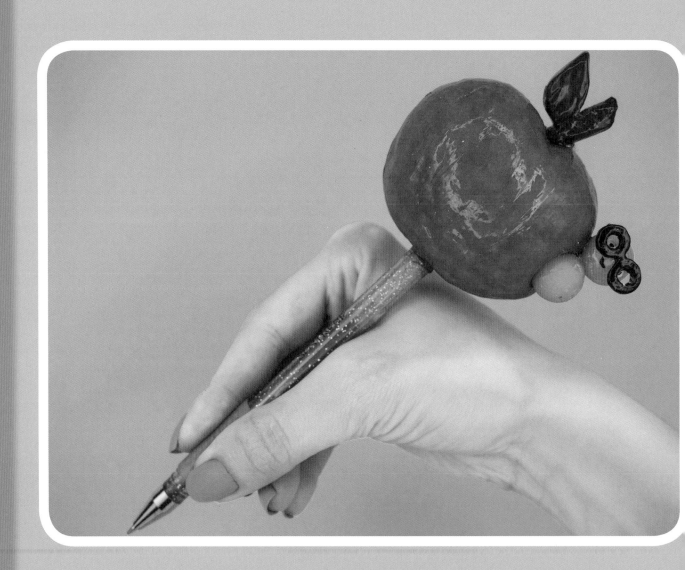

Don't try these projects without adult supervision. Never place any small objects in your mouth. Some materials can be toxic if you contact, inhale, or eat them. Also, tools can be potentially hazardous if used incorrectly.

11. APPLE PEN WITH BOOKWORM

Sometimes you don't need a complex recipe to make a squishy. In fact, it only takes some moisturized air-dry clay to create one.

Materials

- 1 sponge
- Super glue
- PVA glue
- Acrylic paint (red, green, brown, black)
- 3 beads
- 1 sheet of cardboard

 Take a sponge and cut it into the shape of an apple. (Caution: Scissors are sharp! Please use under adult supervision.)

2 Smooth the surface using scissors.

3 Glue it to the end of a pen.

4 Mix some acrylic paint with an equal amount of any glue, such as transparent paper glue.

5 Cover the apple with a thick layer of the mix. Give it some time to dry and then apply a second layer.

6 Draw a branch and a leaf on a piece of sponge and cut it out.

 7

Paint the branch and the leaf with the mix of paint and glue.

 8

When the details dry, glue it to the top of the apple.

 9

Make a small hole in the side of the toy.

10

Paint two small spheres of sponge green and glue them right where the hole is.

 Draw and cut glasses using thick cardboard that will fit on the worm's head.

 Apply a thick layer of any paint to the glasses.

 Glue the glasses to the second sphere where the worm's head is (second sphere furthest from the hole).

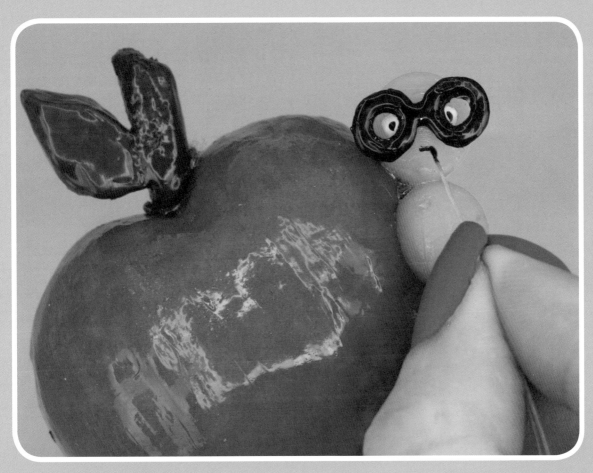

 Paint a funny face, and you are done!

Let it dry and then it'll be ready for use!

Don't try these projects without adult supervision. Never place any small objects in your mouth. Some materials can be toxic if you contact, inhale, or eat them. Also, tools can be potentially hazardous if used incorrectly.

12. MOCHI CLOUD

Squishies originated in Japan as popular toys, but their reach has spread around the world! Mochi, a Japanese rice cake, is another product of Japan and has made its way across the globe. So, let's make a kawaii squishy cloud with a squishy DIY kit from Japan!

Materials

- Gel hardness set for squishies
- Acrylic paint (pink, white, and black)
- A silicone baking mold (store-bought or self-made)
- PVA or transparent glue

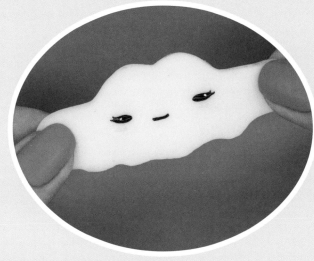

1 For this project, we'll use the DIY kit which you can buy on any Japanese online hobby shop or on Amazon, Etsy, etc. The kit consists of two liquids: a white one and a transparent one.

2 First, pour the white liquid into the container, and then add the transparent liquid in a 3:1 ratio.

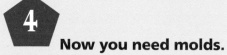

3 Mix until it becomes a uniform mass.

4 Now you need molds.

5 The easiest way to make a mold yourself is to cut a silhouette out from a thick piece of cardboard. (Caution: Scissors are sharp! Please use under adult supervision.)

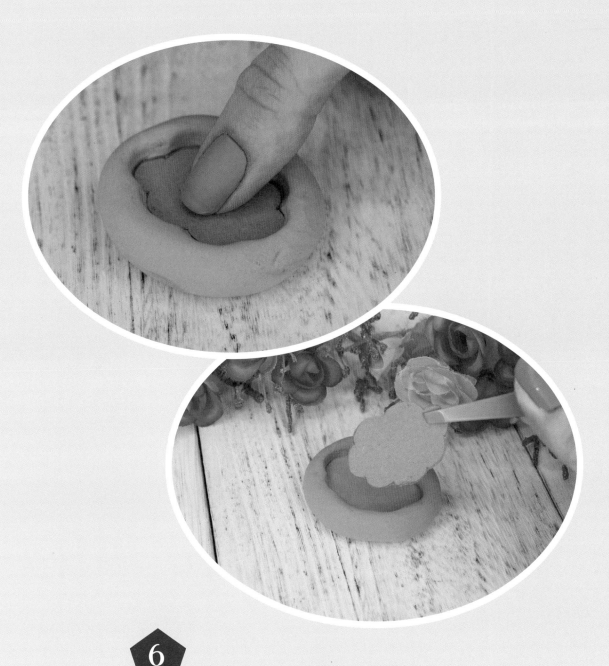

6

Press the template on a piece
of air-dry clay. When it hardens,
use it as the mold.

Pour the resin-like mass into the mold.

After 1–2 days, when the mass hardens, cover it with powder from the set so that the toy doesn't stick to your hands.

The final step is to add eyes and a smile. For this, mix equal amounts of acrylic paint and glue together. The glue helps the paint to stay flexible. This is particularly important on the surface of the squishy toy since it stretches so much and you don't want the paint to crack and fall off.

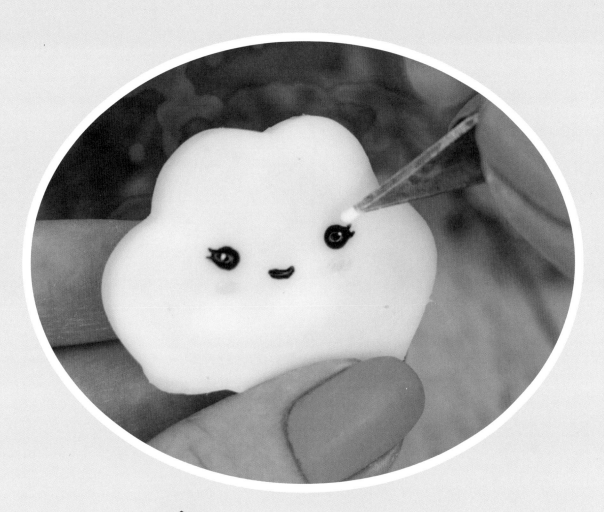

10 Paint the cute face. When it dries, you can play with it.

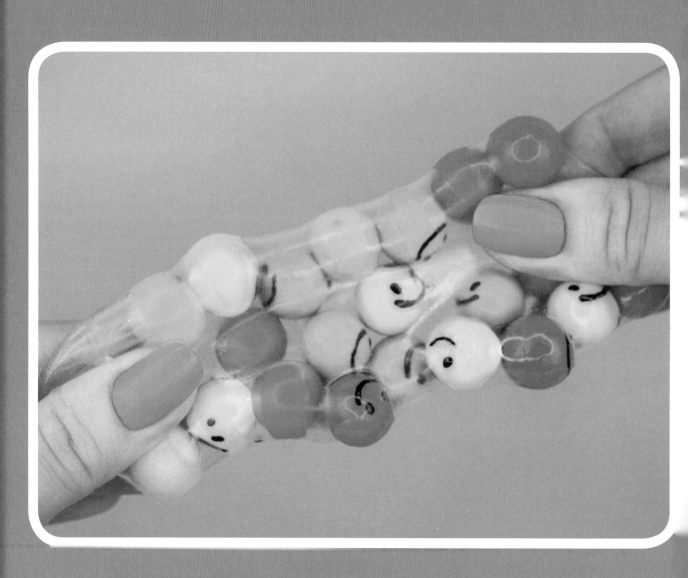

Don't try these projects without adult supervision. Never place any small objects in your mouth. Some materials can be toxic if you contact, inhale, or eat them. Also, tools can be potentially hazardous if used incorrectly.

13. Liquid Emoji

This toy is an anti-stress toy, it's liquid, and it has smileys. What could be better, right?

Materials

- Polymer clay or silicone (pink, green, yellow, and black)
- 1 plastic bottle
- 1 transparent balloon
- Baby oil

1 Create pink, green, yellow, and black masses from either a polymer clay or, better yet, a silicone mass you made yourself (how to make a silicone mass is described in detail in the "Smart Cookie" project on page 45).

2 Make spheres of the same size from the pink, green, and yellow masses.

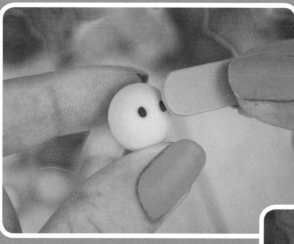

3 Make eyes from the black mass.

4 From the same black mass, create smiles.

5 Cut off the top portion of the plastic bottle. (Caution: Scissors are sharp! Please use under adult supervision.)

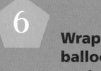

6 Wrap a transparent balloon around the part you cut.

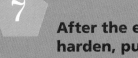 **7** After the emoji spheres harden, put them into the balloon.

 8 Pour some baby oil into the transparent balloon.

9 Finally, tie the balloon and cut off the end.

This fun toy is very calming and satisfying.

Don't try these projects without adult supervision. Never place any small objects in your mouth. Some materials can be toxic if you contact, inhale, or eat them. Also, tools can be potentially hazardous if used incorrectly.

14. BUNNY POPSICLE

This is a great summer toy that can be used as a charm or a decoration for a backpack.

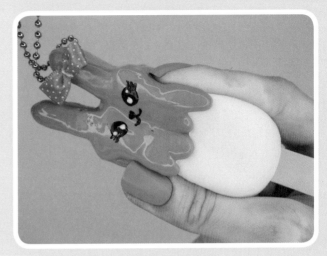

 1

On a sponge, draw an outline of a popsicle with rabbit ears on top.

 2

Take the scissors and cut all the way around it, removing all the excess surrounding the shape you have just drawn. Also, after this, don't forget to "shave away" all the small outstanding bits and edges. Pointed cuticle scissors are the best for this task.
(Caution: Scissors are sharp! Please use under adult supervision.)

 Cover the sponge with some modeling air-dry clay. This kind of clay still stays soft even after it dries, so it's great for this project.

 Cover the top of the toy with fabric paint. Hold the toy at a small angle, so that drops of paint slowly flow down the sides.

 Create a hole at the bottom of the toy.

6 Add some super glue to the hole.

Glue the popsicle stick in the hole.

When the paint dries, draw a face with white and black fabric paints. It is not necessary, but you can glue a decorative element to an ear, such as a bow.

Make a hole at the top of the toy.

10 The last step is to transform it into an accessory by adding it to a chain or keyring, if you like.

You can either make this toy in a smaller size and use it as a charm or decor for a backpack, or you can make a larger toy to play with.

Don't try these projects without adult supervision. Never place any small objects in your mouth. Some materials can be toxic if you contact, inhale, or eat them. Also, tools can be potentially hazardous if used incorrectly.

15. FUNNY CACTUS

Do you have a lot of paints, markers, etc.? Do you also love painting?! Then this project is for you. This original squishy is easy, quick, and super cool.

Materials

- Pencils, paints, or markers
- 1 sheet of paper
- Clear tape
- Cotton, plastic bags, or pieces of a sponge

1 Draw or paint this funny cactus using colored pencils, markers, or paints. Do not worry if you have trouble drawing or painting; put a sheet of paper over the picture in the book and trace it.

2 The second picture, which you need to prepare yourself, is the back part of the cactus. There are two options: you can draw and paint it or you can simply draw a cactus silhouette on a piece of green paper.

3 Cut out the front and back of the cactus. (Caution: Scissors are sharp! Please use under adult supervision.)

4 Take some clear tape and apply it to the paper. This is needed so that when we squeeze our squishy toy, the paper won't crinkle or rip.

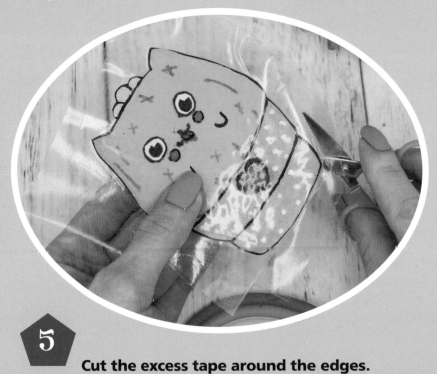

5 Cut the excess tape around the edges.

6

Now, tape up the edges so that you essentially create a pocket. Make sure to leave a small part of it open so that you can put some filling in.

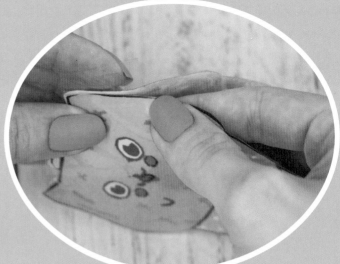

7

Fill the toy with the cotton, cut-up plastic bags, or pieces of a sponge.

8

Tape up the opening and you're finished.

This project is super quick and simple to make, and it's a lot of fun.

ALSO AVAILABLE